MS-DOS®
COMMANDS
R E V I S E D

Including Version 3.3

Microsoft
P R E S S

VA**N** WOLVERTON, author of *Running MS-DOS*

PUBLISHED BY
Microsoft Press
A Division of Microsoft Corporation
16011 NE 36th Way, Box 97017
Redmond, Washington 98073-9717

Library of Congress Cataloging in Publication Data
Wolverton, Van, 1939-
Quick reference guide to MS-DOS commands.
1. MS-DOS (Computer operating system)   2. IBM Personal
Computer—Programming.
I. Title.
QA76.76.063W64   1988   005.4'46   86-31146
ISBN 1-55615-182-9

Printed and bound in the United States of America.

1 2 3 4 5 6 7 8 9 WAKWAK 3 2 1 0 9 8

Distributed to the book trade in the United States by Harper & Row.

Distributed to the book trade in Canada by General Publishing
Company, Ltd.

Distributed to the book trade outside the United States and Canada
by Penguin Books Ltd.

Penguin Books Ltd., Harmondsworth, Middlesex, England
Penguin Books Australia Ltd., Ringwood, Victoria, Australia
Penguin Books N.Z. Ltd., 182-190 Wairau Road, Auckland 10,
New Zealand

British Cataloging in Publication Data available

Project Editor: Suzanne Viescas
Technical Editor: David Rygmyr

CONTENTS

INTRODUCTION v
DOS COMMANDS 1
BATCH COMMANDS 63
CONFIGURATION COMMANDS 71
EDLIN COMMANDS 79
INDEX 87

INTRODUCTION

This quick reference guide contains commands for DOS versions 2.0 through 3.3. DOS, batch, configuration, and Edlin commands are presented in alphabetic order within these groups. Each entry includes the full form of the command, a brief description of the command and its parameters, and usually an example of its use.

Some commands have many possible forms. When you must enter parameters exactly, they are shown precisely as you must type them. When a parameter is shown in *italic,* it represents a variable that you must supply, such as the name of a file, disk drive, or output device. Items in brackets are optional, and you include them only under specific circumstances. The ¦ symbol means that you should choose only one of the options within the brackets. DO NOT TYPE THE BRACKETS OR THE ¦ SYMBOL.

The parameters for DOS commands that you will encounter in this quick reference guide include the following:

drive:	A letter referring to a disk drive, followed by a required colon.
filename	The name of a file, usually followed by an extension. For example: `report.jan`
path	One or more directory names, each separated from the previous one by a backslash (\). For example: `\mkt\reports`
pathname	One or more directory names followed by a filename, each name separated from the previous one by a backslash (\). For example: `\mkt\reports\report.jan`
switches	Controls for commands, each beginning with a slash (/). For example: `/p`

DOS COMMANDS

The system prompt (such as A> or C>) tells you that DOS is at the command level, ready to accept commands. The letter in the system prompt identifies the current drive; you can change the current drive by typing the new drive letter, followed by a colon, and pressing the Enter key.

If you make an error typing a command, you can press the Backspace key to erase the last letter typed. When you have typed the command correctly, execute it by pressing the Enter key.

Append

Syntax:

append [/x][/e]
or
append [*drive:*][*path*][;[*drive:*][*path*] . . .]

Description:

Tells DOS to look for data files in the specified drive and directory.

/x makes the Append data path available to other DOS commands. You can use /x only the first time you enter an Append command after starting DOS. If you specify /x, you cannot specify *drive:path*; you must enter another Append command to define the data path.

/e makes the Append data path part of the DOS environment. You can use /e only the first time you enter an Append command after starting DOS. If you specify /e, you cannot specify *drive:path*; you must enter another Append command to define the data path.

The /x and /e switches are available only in version 3.3.

drive: is the drive to be searched. If you omit *drive:*, DOS assumes the current drive.

path is the name of the directory or subdirectory to be searched. You can enter more than one *drive:path* by separating them with semicolons.

An Append command followed only by a semicolon removes any search paths previously set with Append.

An Append command with no parameters displays the current search path for data files.

Warning: When an assigned drive is to be part of the search path, you must use the Assign command before the Append command.

Example:

To set the search path for data files to include the \LETTERS and \REPORTS directories on drive B and the \MEMOS directory on drive A, type:

```
append b:\letters;b:\reports;a:\memos
```

Assign

Syntax:

assign [*drive1=drive2* [. . .]]

Description:

Refers requests for one disk drive to another disk drive.

drive1 is the drive you don't want to use (the letter to be assigned to a different drive).

drive2 is the drive that is to be used in place of *drive1*.

Multiple drive assignments can be made with a single Assign command.

If you type Assign alone, DOS cancels any assignments currently in effect.

This command is available in PC-DOS versions 2.X and later, and in MS-DOS versions 3.0 and later.

Warning: Because Assign affects *all* requests for a drive, you should use it with caution, especially if the reassignment involves a fixed disk. Always bear in mind that some DOS commands, such as Erase, delete existing files from the disk in the specified drive. The Assign command also hides drive characteristics from programs that require detailed knowledge of the drive size and format, such as Backup, Restore,

Label, Join, Substitute, or Print. The Format, Diskcopy, Diskcomp, and System commands ignore any drive reassignments made with Assign.

Example:

Suppose you have a graphics program that requires all data files to be on drive B, but you want to use your fixed disk (drive C) for data files. To tell DOS to assign all requests for drive B to drive C instead, type:

```
assign b=c
```

Attribute

Syntax:

attrib [+r¦−r] [+a¦−a] [*drive:*]*pathname* [/s]

Description:

Lets you protect files by making them read-only (unable to be changed or erased), or, in version 3.2 and 3.3, allows you to set or remove a file's archive flag for use with the Backup or Xcopy command.

+r tells DOS to make the file read-only.

−r tells DOS to let the file be changed or erased.

+a tells DOS to set the file's archive flag.

−a tells DOS to remove the file's archive flag.

drive:pathname is the name and location of the file whose read-only or archive flag status is to be displayed or changed. Wildcard characters are permitted.

/s tells Attribute to process all subdirectories in *pathname*.

If you enter the Attrib command with only a pathname, Attrib displays the name of the file, preceded by an *R* if the file is read-only and, in versions 3.2 and 3.3, preceded by an *A* if the file's archive bit is set.

This command is available only in versions 3.0 and later.

Examples:

To make BANK.TXT (in the current drive and directory) a read-only file, type:

```
attrib +r bank.txt
```

To remove the read-only protection, type:

```
attrib -r bank.txt
```

To set the archive flag on all files in the directory \SYSTEM on drive C, including all files stored in subdirectories of \SYSTEM, type:

```
attrib +a c:\system\*.* /s
```

Backup

Syntax:

backup [*drive:*][*pathname*] *drive*: [/s][/m][/a][/p][/f][/d:*date*] [/L:*filename*][/t:*time*]

Description:

Makes backup copies of files from one disk to another; erases files already on the target disk, unless you include the /a switch. If you back up files to a hard disk, creates a \BACKUP directory to store the files in.

drive:pathname is the name and location of the files to be backed up. Wildcard characters are permitted. If you do not specify a path, Backup assumes the current directory. If you do not specify a filename, Backup backs up all files in that directory.

drive: specifies the destination disk to receive the backup files. This parameter is not optional.

/s backs up the contents of all subdirectories.

/m backs up only those files modified since the last backup.

/a adds the file(s) to existing files on the destination disk (does not erase the destination disk).

/p packs the destination disk with as many files as possible, even if a subdirectory must be created to hold some of the files. (Available only in MS-DOS versions 2.0 through 3.1.)

/f formats the target disk if it isn't already formatted. For this switch to work, the Format command must be accessible via the current command path.

/d:*date* backs up only those files modified on or after *date*. The date format depends on whether the Country command is in effect; the default is *mm-dd-yy*.

/L:*filename* creates a log file in the root directory of the source disk. If you do not specify a filename, Backup creates a file named BACKUP.LOG and places the log entries there.

/t:*time* backs up only those files modified on or after *time*. The time format depends on whether the Country command is in effect; the default is *hh:mm:ss*. (Not supported in all implementations of Backup.)

The /p, /t:*time*, and /L:*filename* switches are not supported by PC-DOS.

PC-DOS versions 3.0 and later and MS-DOS versions 3.1 and later support any combination of media.

Note: You should not use Backup with a drive affected by a Join command; if you do, you may not be able to restore the files with the Restore command. You should also not use Backup with a drive affected by an Append, Assign, or Substitute command.

Example:

To back up all the files in \MKT\BUDGET from the current drive to drive B, type:

```
backup \mkt\budget b:
```

Backup then prompts you to check that the correct disk is in the drive. Backup also prompts you to insert additional disks if the disk in drive B becomes full.

Break

Syntax:

break [on ¦ off]

Description:

Tells the operating system how often to check for a Ctrl-C, the key sequence you use to terminate a program or batch file.

By default, DOS checks for Ctrl-C when reading from or writing to a character device, such as a printer, screen, or auxiliary port. The Break on command instructs DOS to also check for Ctrl-C each time a disk is read from or written to.

If you type Break alone, Break displays a message informing you whether Break is on or off.

Examples:

To have DOS also check for a Ctrl-C whenever it reads from or writes to a disk, type:

`break on`

To restore the default condition, type:

`break off`

Change Code Page

Syntax:

chcp [*nnn*]

Description:

Changes or displays the number of the code page that DOS uses for all devices that support code-page switching.

nnn is the number of the new code page:

Code-page number	Code page
437	United States
850	Multilingual
860	Portuguese
863	French-Canadian
865	Nordic

If you omit *nnn*, Change Code Page displays the current (active) page. The current code page is the character set DOS uses to display characters. Chcp displays an error message if the specified code page isn't compatible with a device or if the specified code page wasn't prepared with the *codepage prepare* parameter of the Mode command.

Note: You must execute the National Language Support Function (Nlsfunc) before you can use the Change Code Page command.

Examples:

To change the current code page to Nordic (assuming it's already been prepared), type:

```
chcp 865
```

To display the current code page, type:

```
chcp
```

Assuming the first example was successful, Chcp displays:

```
Active code page: 865
```

Change Directory

Syntax:

chdir [*drive:*][*path*]

Description:

Displays the name of, or changes, the current directory. (Can be abbreviated as cd.)

drive: can be used to change the current directory on another drive to *path*. This parameter does not cause the system to change drives, and the directory from which you entered the command will remain the current directory. If you enter *drive:* without a *path*, the current directory on *drive:* is displayed.

path is the name of the directory that is to become the current directory. If *path* includes one or more subdirectories, you must precede each one with a backslash.

If you enter Chdir without parameters, it displays the current directory of the current drive.

Examples:

To change the current directory to the directory named \DATA, type:

```
cd \data
```

To change to the \LETTERS subdirectory of the \WORD directory, type:

```
cd \WORD\LETTERS
```

To back up one directory level closer to the root directory, type:

`cd ..`

To change to the root directory, type:

`cd \`

Check Disk

Syntax:

chkdsk [*drive:*][*pathname*] [/v][/f]

Description:

Analyzes the allocation of storage on a disk and displays a summary report of the space occupied by files and directories, the number of bytes in bad sectors, the number of bytes free, and the total system memory. Also displays a message informing you whether noncontiguous files were found.

drive:pathname is the name and location of the file to be checked. Wildcard characters are permitted. If you omit *drive:*, Chkdsk assumes the current drive. If you omit *pathname*, Chkdsk checks the entire disk.

/v displays the name of each directory and file on the disk as it checks.

/f tells Chkdsk to correct any errors it finds, after prompting for permission. If you do not include the /f switch, Chkdsk does not convert lost chains into clusters, even if you respond *y* to the prompt.

Note: You cannot use Chkdsk with a drive affected by a Join or Substitute command or with a drive assigned to a network.

Example:

To check all files on the disk in drive B and display the directory and filenames, type:

`chkdsk b:*.* /v`

Clear Screen

Syntax:

cls

Description:

Clears the screen and displays the system prompt.

Example:

To erase everything on the screen and display the system prompt in the upper left corner, type:

cls

Command Processor

Syntax:

command [*drive:*][*path*] [*cttydev*][/e:*nnnnn*][/p][/c *string*]

Description:

Allows you to invoke a copy of the parent command processor and, optionally, change some of its characteristics. (The command processor is the part of DOS that issues prompts, interprets commands and batch files, and loads and executes application programs.)

drive:path specifies the drive and/or the directory to be searched for COMMAND.COM when its transient portion needs to be reloaded.

cttydev specifies a character device to be used for input and output instead of the default keyboard and monitor. (Not available in PC-DOS.)

/e:*nnnnn* specifies the initial size, in bytes, of the command processor's environment block (versions 3.2 and 3.3). The maximum size is 32768 bytes; the default is 160 bytes. The number is rounded up to the next paragraph boundary (evenly divisible by 16) if appropriate.

/p disables the Exit command and causes the newly loaded command processor to be fixed permanently in memory.

/c *string* causes the secondary command processor to behave as a transient program. It executes the command or program specified by *string* and then exits and returns control to the parent processor. If you do not include /c *string* in the command line, then the secondary copy of COMMAND.COM remains in memory until an Exit command is executed. When used in combination with other switches, this must be the last switch on the command line.

Examples:

To execute the batch file MENU2.BAT from the batch file MENU1.BAT and then resume execution of MENU1.BAT, include the following line in MENU1.BAT:

```
command /c menu2
```

Note: The technique in this example is unnecessary with version 3.3, which includes the Call batch file command.

To load a secondary command processor permanently into memory and transfer the input and output device to a terminal attached to a serial port, type:

```
command aux /p
```

Compare

Syntax:

comp [*drive:*][*pathname1*] [*drive:*][*pathname2*]

Description:

Compares two files or sets of files to see if their contents are the same. This command is available in all versions of PC-DOS and in MS-DOS version 3.3.

drive:pathname1 and *drive:pathname2* are the names and locations of the files to be compared. Wildcard characters are permitted. If you include no drive or path, Compare assumes the current directory of the current. If you omit either or both filenames, Compare prompts you for the information.

Example:

To compare REPORT.TXT on drive B with BUDGET.FEB on drive A, type:

```
comp b:report.txt a:budget.feb
```

Copy: Combine Files

Syntax:

copy [*drive:*][*path*]*source*[+[[*drive:*][*path*]*source*] . . .]
[*drive:*][*path*]*target* [/a][/b][/v]

Description:

Combines two or more source files into the specified target file, creating *target* if it doesn't already exist, or concatenates one or more source files onto the first source file specified in the command line.

drive:path source is the name and location of the files to be combined. Wildcard characters are permitted. You can also specify a list of several filenames separated by plus signs (+).

Caution: If any file in a list separated by plus signs doesn't exist, Copy goes on to the next name without telling you the file doesn't exist.

drive:path target is the name and location of the file that results from combining the source files. If you specify *target*, Copy combines the source files into *target*. If you omit *target*, Copy combines the source files into the first source file.

/a indicates that the file is an ASCII (text-only) file. Applied to *source* files, /a copies data up to, but not including, the first Control-Z character encountered in each file. Applied to *target*, /a appends a Control-Z character to the *target* file as the last character in the file.

/b indicates that the file is a binary file.

/v performs read-after-write verification of destination file(s).

Note: The /a and /b switches affect the filename immediately preceding them and all subsequent filenames in the command line, until another /a or /b switch is encountered.

Warning: When Copy concatenates to the first source file in a series, the original (unconcatenated) version of that file is lost.

Examples:

To combine BANK.DOC and REPORT.DOC into a new file named BANKRPT.DOC (while keeping the originals intact), type:

```
copy bank.doc+report.doc bankrpt.doc
```

To concatenate BUDGET.FEB and BUDGET.MAR into the existing source file BUDGET.JAN, type:

```
copy budget.jan+budget.feb+budget.mar
```

Copy: Copy from a Device

Syntax:

copy *source target*

Description:

Copies the output of a device to a file or another device.

source is the name of the device whose output is to be copied.

target is the name of the file or device to which the output is to be copied. If *target* is a filename, it can include a path.

Warning: Be sure that both the source and target devices exist; if you try to copy to or from a device that doesn't exist or isn't ready, DOS may stop running, forcing you to restart the system.

Examples:

To copy from the keyboard (CON) to the printer (PRN), be sure the printer is turned on and then type:

```
copy con prn
```

To copy from the keyboard (CON) to a file named MYFILE.TXT, type:

```
copy con myfile.txt
```

In both examples, when you have finished typing the file, you must press F6 or Ctrl-Z and then Enter to terminate the Copy command.

Copy: Copy a File to a Device

Syntax:

copy [*drive:*]*pathname device* [/a][/b]

Description:

Copies a file to a device.

drive:pathname is the name and location of the file to be sent to a device. Wildcard characters are permitted.

device is the name of the device to which *pathname* is to be sent.

/a indicates that the file is an ASCII (text-only) file. When used, /a copies data from *pathname* up to, but not including, the first Control-Z character encountered in the file.

/b indicates that the file is a binary file.

You cannot use the Copy command to send output to COM or AUX serial ports.

Warning: Be sure *device* exists; if you try to send a file to a device that doesn't exist or isn't ready, DOS may stop running, forcing you to restart the system.

Examples:

To send a copy of each file in the current drive and directory and with the extension .TXT to the printer, type:

```
copy *.txt prn
```

To send a copy of the file REPORT.TXT to the screen, type:

```
copy report.txt con
```

Copy: Copy a File to a File

Syntax:

copy [*drive:*]*pathname1* [*drive:*][*pathname2*] [/a][/b][/v]

Description:

Copies a file to another file.

drive:pathname1 is the name and location of the source file.
drive:pathname2 is the name and location of the target file. Wildcard characters are permitted in both filenames.

If you specify a drive other than the current drive for *pathname1* and omit *drive: pathname2*, *pathname1* is copied to the current directory of the current drive. If you specify only a drive letter for *pathname2*, *pathname1* is copied to the disk in the drive you specify and given the same filename.

If *pathname1* doesn't exist, Copy displays the pathname you specified, followed by *File not found* and *0 File(s) copied* and returns to command level. If *pathname2* doesn't exist, Copy creates it. If *pathname2* already exists, Copy replaces its contents with those of *pathname1*.

Warning: This latter situation is the same as erasing the existing file, so be careful not to make a copy of a file and give the copy the same name as an existing file that you want to keep.

/a indicates that the file is an ASCII (text-only) file. Applied to *pathname1*, /a copies data up to, but not including, the first Control-Z character encountered. Applied to *pathname2*, /a appends a Control-Z character to the file as the last character of the new file.

/b indicates that the file is a binary file.

/v performs read-after-write verification of destination file(s).

Note: The /a and /b switches affect the filename immediately preceding them and all subsequent filenames in the command line, until another /a or /b switch is encountered.

Examples:

To make a copy of the file REPORT.DOC on the same disk and name the copy RESULTS.DOC, type:

```
copy report.doc results.doc
```

To copy the file REPORT.DOC from drive A to the current drive, giving the file the same name, type:

```
copy a:report.doc
```

To copy the file REPORT.DOC from the current drive to the disk in drive A, giving the file the same name, type:

```
copy report.doc a:
```

Ctty (Change I/O Device)

Syntax:

ctty *device*

Description:

Specifies the character device to be used as the standard input and standard output device.

device is a logical character device name (AUX, COM1, COM2, or CON).

DOS ordinarily uses the computer's built-in keyboard and screen as the standard input and standard output device. Ctty allows you to assign another character device as the standard device instead.

Examples:

To redirect keyboard input and screen output to a terminal attached to a serial port (AUX), type:

```
ctty aux
```

To restore control to the console (CON, the computer's built-in keyboard and screen), type:

```
ctty con
```

Date

Syntax:

date [*month-day-year*]

Description:

Sets the system calendar.

month is a number from 1 through 12.

day is a number from 1 through 31.

year is a number from 80 through 99 (for 1980 through 1999). If you use four digits to enter the year, you can enter dates through 12-31-2099.

If you don't include any parameters, Date displays the current setting of the system calendar and prompts you to enter a date.

Note: In MS-DOS versions 2.1 and later and in PC-DOS 3.0 and later, if a Country command was used in the CONFIG.SYS file when the system was started, or, in MS-DOS version 3.3 or PC-DOS version 3.0 and later, if the Select command was used to configure a country-specific system disk, the format for the date may be different.

Example:

To set the system date to January 1, 1987, type:

```
date 1-1-87
```

Delete

Syntax:

del [*drive:*]*pathname*

Description:

Deletes a file or group of files.

drive:pathname is the name and location of the file or group of files to be deleted. Wildcard characters are permitted. If you omit *drive:*, Delete assumes the current drive.

You cannot use Delete to delete a directory. (See Remove Directory.)

Warning: The action of the Delete command is final, so be sure you have typed the correct drive letter and extension before you press Enter.

Example:

To delete all files in the \OLD directory on drive B with a .TXT extension, type:

```
del b:\old\*.txt
```

Directory

Syntax:

dir [*drive:*][*path*][*filename*] [/w][/p]

Description:

Displays a directory listing of files on a disk, the number of files in the specified directory, and the number of bytes available on the disk.

drive: is the drive on which the directory to be listed is located. If you specify only *drive:*, Dir displays all files in the current directory of that drive.

path is the name of the directory whose files are to be displayed.

filename is the name of a specific file to be listed. Only the entry for that file is displayed. Wildcard characters are permitted.

If Dir is entered with no parameters, the entries for all files in the current directory of the current drive are displayed.

/w displays filenames and extensions only, in five columns across the screen.

/p displays the entries one screenful at a time.

Examples:

To display the current directory of drive C in the wide format, type:

```
dir c: /w
```

To display the directory of \LETTERS on drive B one screenful at a time, type:

```
dir b:\letters /p
```

Disk Compare

Syntax:

diskcomp [*drive1:* [*drive2:*]] [/1][/8]

Description:

Compares two entire floppy disks. (See Compare or File Compare for comparing sets of files.)

drive1: and *drive2:* are the drives containing the floppy disks to be compared. If you omit *drive2:*, Diskcomp compares the floppy disk in *drive1:* to the floppy disk in the current drive. If you omit both drives, Diskcomp assumes you want to use only the current drive and prompts you to switch floppy disks during the comparison.

/1 compares only the first sides of floppy disks, even if the disks and drives are double-sided.

/8 limits the comparison to the first 8 sectors per track, even if the floppy disk in *drive1:* has 9 or 15 sectors per track.

This command is available in PC-DOS versions 2.0 and later and in MS-DOS versions 3.2 and 3.3.

Note: You cannot use Diskcomp to compare disks of different types (such as 360 KB with 1.2 MB). In addition, you cannot use Diskcomp with a fixed disk; with a drive affected by a Substitute command; or with a drive assigned to a network. You should not use Diskcomp with a drive affected by a Join command. Diskcomp ignores assignments made with an Assign command.

Examples:

With a two-floppy-disk-drive system, to compare the disk in drive A and the disk in drive B, type:

```
diskcomp a: b:
```

With a single-disk-drive system, type:

```
diskcomp
```

and follow the prompts.

To compare the disk in drive B to the disk in the current drive, type:

```
diskcomp b:
```

Disk Copy

Syntax:

diskcopy [*drive1:*] [*drive2:*] [/1]

Description:

Makes a duplicate of a floppy disk.

drive1: is the drive that contains the floppy disk to be copied.

drive2: is the drive that contains the floppy disk that is to receive the copy. If you omit *drive2:*, Diskcopy copies the disk in *drive1:* to the floppy disk in the current drive.

/1 copies only the first side of a floppy disk. (Available only in PC-DOS and in MS-DOS versions 3.2 and 3.3.)

PC-DOS versions of Diskcopy format the disk in *drive2:* before copying; MS-DOS versions of Diskcopy prior to 3.2 require that you first format the target disk.

PC-DOS versions give the floppy disk in *drive2:* the same number of sides and sectors per track as the floppy disk in *drive1:*. If the floppy disk in *drive1:* has 9 sectors per track and the floppy disk in *drive2:* was already formatted with 8 sectors per track, Diskcopy reformats the floppy disk in *drive2:* to 9 sectors before copying.

You cannot use Diskcopy to copy to a disk of a different type (such as 360 KB to 1.2 MB).

Note: You cannot use Diskcopy with a drive affected by the Substitute command or with a drive assigned to a network. You should not use Diskcopy with a drive affected by the Join command. Diskcopy ignores drive reassignments made by the Assign command.

Examples:

With a two-floppy-disk-drive system, to copy the disk in drive A to the disk in drive B, type:

```
diskcopy a: b:
```

With a single-disk-drive system, type:

```
diskcopy
```

and follow the prompts.

Erase

Syntax:

erase [*drive:*]*pathname*

Description:

Erases one or more files.

drive:pathname is the name and location of the file or group of files to be deleted. Wildcard characters are permitted. If you omit *drive:*, Erase assumes the current drive.

You cannot use Erase to delete a directory. (See Remove Directory.)

Warning: The action of the Erase command is final, so be sure you have typed the correct filename and the correct drive letter and extension before you press Enter.

Examples:

To erase the file named BUDGET.APR on the disk in the current drive, type:

```
erase budget.apr
```

To erase all files with an extension of .TXT on the floppy disk in drive B, type:

```
erase b:*.txt
```

Exe2bin (Executable to Binary Conversion)

Syntax:

exe2bin [*drive:*]*pathname1* [*drive:*][*pathname2*]

Description:

Converts an executable file (a file with a .EXE extension) to a binary-image file (a file with a .BIN extension). If the executable file meets certain requirements, you can rename the resulting binary-image file as a command file (a file with a .COM extension); it will then run faster than its .EXE counterpart. This is an advanced DOS command, and you should refer to the documentation that came with your operating system before you attempt to use it.

Exit

Syntax:

exit

Description:

Terminates a secondary copy of the command processor invoked by the Command command. Control returns to the parent program or command processor from which the Command command was issued.

Exit has no effect if the secondary command processor was loaded with the /p (permanent) switch or if it is the original command processor (the one loaded when the computer is turned on or restarted with Ctrl-Alt-Del).

Fastopen

Syntax:

fastopen [*drive:*[=*nnn*] [. . .]]

Description:

Reduces access time to frequently used files by having DOS maintain a list of their names and locations. (Available only in version 3.3.)

drive: is the letter of the drive whose files and subdirectories you want DOS to remember. *drive:* must refer to a fixed disk.

nnn is a number in the range 10 through 999. The default for PC-DOS is 34; the default for MS-DOS is 10.

You can specify a maximum of four fixed disks in a single Fastopen command.

You can use the Fastopen command only once per session. If you then want to change the Fastopen settings again, you must restart DOS. Note that Fastopen uses approximately 40 bytes of memory for the name and location of each file in the list.

Each time you open a file, Fastopen adds that file's name and location to the list. If the list is full, the name and location of the oldest accessed file is dropped from the list. Thus, if a particular file is accessed frequently, its name and location will probably be on the list.

Note: You cannot use Fastopen with a drive affected by a Join, Assign, or Substitute command or with a drive assigned to a network.

Example:

To tell DOS to keep a list of the names and locations of the last 70 files accessed on drive C, type:

```
fastopen c:=70
```

File Compare

Syntax:

fc [/b][/#][/a][/c][/L][/Lb *n*][/n][/t][/w][/*nnnn*]
[*drive:*]*pathname1* [*drive:*]*pathname2*

Description:

Compares two text files containing lines of ASCII text or two binary files containing data of any type. Lists the differences between the two files on the video display.

/b forces a byte-by-byte (binary) comparison; files do not have to be ASCII files. This is the default when the file extension is .EXE, .COM, .SYS, .OBJ, .LIB, or .BIN. You cannot use this switch with any other switch except /*nnnn*.

/# is the number of lines (1 through 9) that must match to resynchronize during an ASCII file comparison. (The default value is 3.)

/a causes abbreviated output of the differences found in an ASCII file comparison.

/c causes case to be ignored when comparing alphabetic characters.

/L forces a line-by-line comparison of two ASCII text files. This is the default when the file extension is not .EXE, .COM, .SYS, .OBJ, .LIB, or .BIN.

/Lb n sets the size of the internal line buffer to n lines. (The default value is 100.)

/n includes line numbers on the output of an ASCII file comparison.

/t causes tabs in text files to be compared literally. (Default is for tabs to be treated as spaces with stops at each eighth character position.)

/w causes leading and trailing spaces and tabs in text file lines to be ignored and consecutive spaces and tabs within a line to be compressed to a single space.

/nnnn is the number of lines that must match to resynchronize during an ASCII file comparison. (The default value is 2.)

drive:pathname1 is the name and location of the first file to be compared.

drive:pathname2 is the name and location of the second file to be compared. Wildcard characters are not permitted in either filename.

This command is available only in MS-DOS. The /# switch is available only in versions 2.X and 3.0. The /a, /L, /Lb n, /n, /t, and /nnnn switches are available only in versions 3.1 and later.

Examples:

To do a line-by-line comparison of the ASCII (text-only) files MYFILE.TXT and YOURFILE.LTR, type:

```
fc myfile.txt yourfile.ltr
```

To force a byte-by-byte comparison of BUDGET.JAN and FORECAST.JAN, type:

```
fc /b budget.jan forecast.jan
```

Find

Syntax:

find [/v][/c][/n] "*string*" [*drive:*][*pathname*][[*drive:*][*pathname*] . . .]

Description:

Searches input lines for a string of characters you specify.

/v displays all lines that do not contain *string*.

/c displays only the total number of lines found.

/n displays each line found, preceded by its line number in the file. This switch is ignored if you use it with /c.

If you enter the Find command with none of these switches, it displays all lines that contain *string*.

string is the string of characters you want to search for. You must enclose the string in quotation marks. The Find command distinguishes between uppercase and lowercase letters.

drive:pathname is the name and location of the file to be searched. If you omit *drive:pathname*, the Find command searches the keyboard input. (You terminate keyboard input by pressing Ctrl-Z or F6.) You can include several different filenames in a single Find command simply by separating them with spaces.

Example:

To display the lines containing *cons* in the file PHONE.TXT (which is on the current drive) and precede each line by a number indicating its position in the file, type:

```
find /n "cons" phone.txt
```

Fixed Disk

Syntax:

fdisk

Description:

Invokes a menu-driven program that allows you to perform hard-disk tasks (such as creating a DOS partition on your hard disk) or to tell DOS which partition is the active partition (the partition DOS should use when initializing the system from the hard disk).

This command is available only in PC-DOS versions 2.0 and later and in MS-DOS version 3.2 and 3.3.

Note: You cannot use Fdisk with a drive affected by a Join or Substitute command, or with a drive assigned to a network.

Example:

To invoke the Fdisk program, type:

```
fdisk
```

Format

Syntax:

format [*drive:*] [/1][/4][/8][/o][/v][/b][/n:*xx*][/t:*yy*][/s]

Description:

Prepares a disk so that DOS can store files on it and erases any existing data on the disk. You can make a system disk (a disk capable of booting the system) by using the /s switch.

drive: is the drive that contains the floppy disk to be formatted. If you omit *drive:*, Format formats the floppy disk in the current drive.

/1 formats only one side of a floppy disk. (Not available in MS-DOS versions 2.0 through 3.1.)

/4 formats a double-sided disk in a high-capacity drive. (Available in PC-DOS versions 3.0 and later and in MS-DOS versions 3.2 and 3.3.)

/8 formats a floppy disk with 8 sectors per track. (Not available in MS-DOS versions 2.0 through 3.1.)

/o formats a disk that is compatible with PC-DOS versions 1.X. (Available only in MS-DOS versions 2.0 through 3.1.)

/v tells Format that you want to give the floppy disk a volume label.

/b formats a disk with 8 sectors per track and allocates space for any version of DOS. DOS is not written to the disk. (See *System.*) This switch cannot be used with /s or /v.

/n:*xx* formats a disk with *xx* sectors per track. (Available only in MS-DOS versions 3.2 and 3.3 and PC-DOS version 3.3.)

/t:*yy* formats a disk with *yy* tracks. (Available only in MS-DOS versions 3.2 and 3.3 and PC-DOS version 3.3.)

/s creates a system (bootable) disk. This must be the last switch on the command line.

The following table shows the valid switches for various types of disks:

Disk type	*Valid switches*
160/180 KB	/1 /4 /8 /b /n:*xx* /t:*yy* /v /s
320/360 KB	/1 /4 /8 /b /n:*xx* /t:*yy* /v /s
720 KB†	/n:*xx* /t:*yy* /v /s
1.2 MB	/n:*xx* /t:*yy* /v /s
1.44 MB†	/n:*xx* /t:*yy* /v /s
fixed disk	/v /s

† 720 KB and 1.44 MB are 3-1/2" disks.

Warning: If you don't specify a drive, you risk formatting your hard disk or system floppy disk. Before you press the Enter key, be sure that you have specified the correct drive. Also, you should not use the Format command with drives affected by a Join or Substitute command. You cannot format disks in a drive assigned to a network. The Format command ignores drive reassignments made with an Assign command.

Examples:

To format the floppy disk in drive B and give it a volume label, type:

```
format b: /v
```

Format prompts you for a volume label after the format operation is completed.

To create a system (bootable) floppy disk in drive B, type:

```
format b: /s
```

Graphics

graphics [*printer*] [/b][/c][/f][/lcd][/p=*port*][/r]

Description:

Enables DOS to print graphics images on any of several types of printers.

printer is an IBM or compatible printer.

Option	Printer type
color1	IBM Personal Computer Color Printer or compatible with a black ribbon
color4	IBM Personal Computer Color Printer or compatible with a red-green-blue-black ribbon
color8	IBM Personal Computer Color Printer or compatible with a cyan-magenta-yellow-black ribbon
compact	IBM Personal Computer Compact Printer or compatible
graphics	IBM Personal Graphics Printer or compatible

If you do not specify *printer*, the default is the IBM Personal Graphics Printer.

/b tells DOS to print the background color as well as the foreground color if you specified *color4* or *color8*. (Not available in PC-DOS versions 2.X.)

/c centers the printout on the printer. This switch works only on a 640x200 image (rotated by default) or on a 320x200 image rotated using the /f switch. (Available only in MS-DOS versions 3.2 and 3.3.)

/f rotates the printout 90 degrees. This switch works only with a 320x200 image. (Available only in MS-DOS versions 3.2 and 3.3.)

/lcd prints the image from the liquid crystal display (LCD) screen of the IBM PC Convertible. (Available only in version 3.3.)

/p=*port* allows the user to specify which port that *printer* is attached to. Valid settings are 1 (LPT1), 2 (LPT2), or 3 (LPT3). The default is 1. (Available only in MS-DOS versions 3.2 and 3.3.)

/r tells DOS to print the screen as you see it—light characters on a dark background. (Not available in PC-DOS versions 2.X.)

After you enter the Graphics command and appropriate parameters, pressing Shift-PrtSc prints everything on the screen of the active display, including graphics images. On a noncolor printer, the Graphics command causes the contents of the screen to print in four shades of gray. You needn't enter the Graphics command again until the next time you start DOS.

Note: Not all printers can print graphics.

Example:

To print graphics images, including the background color, on an IBM Personal Computer Color Printer with a red-green-blue-black ribbon, type:

```
graphics color4 /b
```

Graphics Table

Syntax:

graftabl [*nnn*¦/status¦?]

Description:

Enables DOS to display special graphics characters (ASCII characters 128 through 255) when the Color/Graphics Adapter is in graphics mode.

nnn is the number of the code page whose character set you want to use:

Number	Code page
437	USA Graphics Character Set (default)
850	Multilingual Graphics Character Set
860	Portuguese Graphics Character Set
863	French Canadian Graphics Character Set
865	Nordic Graphics Character Set

/status causes Graftabl to display the active code page. (Can be abbreviated as /sta.)

? causes Graftabl to display a list of the switches you can use with Graftabl.

If you omit all parameters, Graftabl loads the USA character set.

Versions of Graftabl prior to 3.3 do not support any switches. These versions use only one character set, which is built into Graftabl.

This command is available only in PC-DOS versions 3.0 and later and in MS-DOS versions 3.2 and 3.3.

In versions prior to 3.3, you can load Graftabl only once; to disable it, you must reboot the computer.

Examples:

To load the special graphics table (loading the default USA code page in version 3.3), type:

```
graftabl
```

If you have version 3.3 and you want to load the Nordic (Norwegian and Danish) character set or change to the Nordic character set after another character set was previously loaded with a prior Graftabl command, type:

```
graftabl 865
```

Join

Syntax:

join [*drive1: drive2:path*] /d

Description:

Allows the entire directory structure of a drive to be joined, or spliced, into an empty subdirectory of a disk in another drive. After a join, the entire directory structure of the disk in the first drive, starting at the root, together with all files that it contains, appears to be the directory structure of the specified subdirectory on the disk in the second drive; the first drive letter is no longer available.

drive1: is the drive whose entire directory structure will be referenced by *drive2:path*.

drive2:path is the location of the subdirectory to which *drive1:* is to be joined. *path* must be a subdirectory of the root directory of *drive2:*. If *path* already exists, it must be empty; if it doesn't exist, Join creates it.

/d deletes any existing joins that involve *drive1:*. Use this switch only if *drive1:* is the only other parameter in the command line.

If you omit all parameters, Join displays a list of any joins in effect.

The following commands do not work on drives affected by the Join command:

Chkdsk	Format
Diskcomp	Label
Diskcopy	Recover
Fastopen	System
Fdisk	

Note: You cannot use the Join command with a drive assigned to a network.

This command is available only in versions 3.1 and later.

Examples:

If you have an application program that takes up most of a floppy disk and you need a lot of disk space for data files, put the application program disk in drive A and a blank formatted disk in drive B. Then tell DOS to treat the disk in drive B as if it were a directory named \DATA on the disk in drive A by typing:

```
join b: a:\data
```

The join remains in effect until you restart DOS or cancel the join by typing:

```
join b: /d
```

Keyboard

Syntax:

keyb [*xx*[,[*nnn*],[[*drive:*][*pathname*]]]

Description:

Changes the keyboard layout to match a specific language.

This command is not available in versions 2.X and earlier.

In PC-DOS versions 3.0 through 3.2 and MS-DOS version 3.2, the Keyboard command supports only the *xx* parameter, which is not optional. In these versions, *xx* must immediately follow the command with no spaces, for example, keyb*xx* can be one of the following:

xx *code*	*Country*
uk	United Kingdom
gr	Germany
fr	France
it	Italy
sp	Spain

Note: In MS-DOS version 3.2, Keybdv is also available to change to the Dvorak keyboard.

In version 3.3, *xx* is the two-letter keyboard code and *nnn* is the code page for the country whose keyboard layout you want to use. The following parameters are supported:

Keyboard code	*Code page number*†	*Keyboard layout*
us	437	United States (default)
fr	437	France
gr	437	Germany
it	437	Italy
sp	437	Spain
uk	437	United Kingdom
po	860	Portugal
sg	437‡	Swiss-German
sf	437‡	Swiss-French
dk	865	Denmark
be	437‡	Belgium
nl	437	Netherlands
no	865	Norway
la	437	Latin America
sv	437	Sweden
su	437	Finland

† You can use code page number 850 to obtain the multilingual character set in place of the country-specific code place number.

‡ Non-IBM versions only.

Note: You cannot specify a code page that has not been previously prepared with a Mode: Codepage Prepare command.

drive:pathname is the location of KEYBOARD.SYS, the file containing the keyboard layouts. If you do not include this parameter, Keyb looks for the file in the root directory of the system disk.

In versions prior to 3.3, you can load Keyb only once after starting DOS. In version 3.3, you can use subsequent Keyb commands to change to other layouts. In all versions, you can change back to the default keyboard layout (United States) at any time by pressing Ctrl-Alt-F1 and then return to the Keyb layout you loaded by pressing Ctrl-Alt-F2.

Examples:

If you have a version prior to 3.3 and want to change your keyboard layout to match the layout of a French keyboard, simply type:

```
keybfr
```

If you have version 3.3 and want to change to the Norwegian keyboard layout and tell Keyb that the file KEYBOARD.SYS is located in the \DOS directory on drive C, type:

```
keyb no,865,c:\dos\keyboard.sys
```

Label

Syntax:

label [*drive:*][*label*]

Description:

Assigns, changes, or deletes the volume label of a floppy disk or a fixed disk.

drive: is the drive that contains the disk whose volume label is to be altered. If you omit *drive:*, DOS assumes you want to work with the disk in the current drive.

label is the volume label (a maximum of 11 characters) to be assigned to the disk in the drive specified. If you omit *label*, DOS prompts you to enter the new label or press Enter for none. If a label already exists and you chose Enter (for none), DOS asks if you want to delete the current label.

This command is available only in PC-DOS versions 3.0 and later and in MS-DOS versions 3.1 and later.

Note: You cannot use Label with a drive affected by an Assign, Join, or Substitute command or with a drive assigned to a network.

Example:

To assign the volume label DOSDISK to the floppy disk in drive B, type:

```
label b:dosdisk
```

This overwrites any existing label. You do not receive a prompt for confirmation.

Make Directory

Syntax:

mkdir [*drive:*][*path*]*name*

Description:

Creates a directory. (Can be abbreviated md.)

drive: is the drive that contains the disk on which the directory is to be created. If you omit *drive:*, DOS creates the directory on the disk in the current drive.

path is the existing directory in which the new directory will be made. If you omit *path*, DOS creates the new directory in the current directory.

name is the name of the new directory and can be a maximum of eight characters. You must precede *name* by a backslash if you use *path*.

Note: Because the Assign, Join, and Substitute commands can mask the real identities of directories, you shouldn't create directories when those commands are in effect.

Example:

To create the directory \REPORTS in the existing directory \MKT on the disk in drive B, type:

```
md b:\mkt\reports
```

Mode: Align Display (Color/Graphics Adapter)

Syntax:

mode [*display*],*shift*[,t]

Description:

Lets you center the image on a display attached to the Color/Graphics Adapter. Has no effect if you are using an Enhanced Graphics Adapter.

display is one of the values listed under Mode: Select Display. You cannot specify *mono* for the Align Display form of Mode. If you omit *display*, you must still include the comma before *shift*.

shift is either *r* (right) or *l* (left), to shift the image two columns on an 80-column display or one column on a 40-column display.

t causes Mode to display a test pattern. Mode then asks if the screen is aligned properly and shifts it in the direction indicated until you respond that it is.

This form of the Mode command automatically clears the screen.

This command is available in all versions of PC-DOS and in MS-DOS versions 3.2 and 3.3.

Example:

To display 80 columns in color, shift the display 2 columns to the right, and generate a test pattern, type:

```
mode co80,r,t
```

Then respond to the prompt until the display is properly aligned.

Mode: Codepage Prepare

Syntax:

mode *device* codepage prepare=((*nnn*) [*drive:*][*path*]*filename*)

Description:

Prepares one or more code pages for use by a specified device. (Available only in version 3.3.)

device is the name of the device for which the code page is being prepared. Valid *device* names are CON, PRN, LPT1, LPT2, and LPT3.

nnn is the number(s) of the code page(s) to be used with *device*. You must enclose the number(s) within parentheses. You must then enclose the code-page number(s), their parentheses, and *filename* by another set of parentheses. If you specify more than one code-page number, you must separate them with a space. The following code-page numbers are valid:

Code-page number	Code page
437	United States
850	Multilingual
860	Portuguese
863	French-Canadian
865	Nordic

drive:path is the location of *filename*. If you omit *drive:path*, Mode looks in the root directory of the disk used to boot the system for *filename*.

filename is the code-page information (.CPI) file that contains font information for *device*. This parameter is not optional. The following code-page information files are included in PC-DOS version 3.3; versions of MS-DOS 3.3 can contain other files:

EGA.CPI	Enhanced Graphics Adapter (EGA) or IBM PS/2 video adapter
4201.CPI	IBM Proprinter
5202.CPI	IBM Quietwriter III printer
LCD.CPI	IBM PC Convertible liquid crystal display (LCD)

You can abbreviate the word codepage as cp and the word prepare as prep.

Example:

To prepare code pages 437 and 850 for an Enhanced Graphics Display adapter, specifying C:\DOS\EGA.CPI as the code-page information file, type:

```
mode con cp prep=((437 850) c:\dos\ega.cpi)
```

Mode: Codepage Refresh

Syntax:

mode *device* codepage refresh

Description:

Restores a previously selected code page that was erased from memory for a particular device. (Available in version 3.3 only.)

device is the name of the device (CON, PRN, LPT1, LPT2, or LPT3) whose most recently selected code page is being restored.

You can abbreviate codepage as cp and refresh as ref.

Example:

To restore the most recently selected code page for the printer attached to the second parallel printer port, type:

```
mode lpt2 cp ref
```

Mode: Codepage Select

Syntax:

mode *device* codepage select=*nnn*

Description:

Selects a code page for a particular device. (Available in version 3.3 only.)

device is the name of the device for which the code page is being selected. Valid *device* names are CON, PRN, LPT1, LPT2, and LPT3.

nnn is the number of the code page to be used with *device*. The following code page numbers are valid:

Code-page number	Code page	Code-page number	Code page
437	United States	863	French-Canadian
850	Multilingual	865	Nordic
860	Portuguese		

The code page specified by *nnn* must have been previously prepared with a Mode: Codepage Prepare command.

You can abbreviate the word codepage as cp and the word select as sel.

Example:

To select code page 850 for the console, type:

```
mode con cp sel=850
```

Mode: Codepage Status

Syntax:

mode *device* codepage

Description:

Displays the code page status of a particular device. (Available in version 3.3 only.)

device is the name of the device whose code-page status is to be displayed. Valid *device* names are CON, PRN, LPT1, LPT2, and LPT3.

You can abbreviate the word codepage as cp.

Example:

To display the status of the first parallel printer port, type:

```
mode lpt1 cp
```

Mode: Configure Printer

Syntax:

mode LPT*n*[:][*chars*][,[*lines*][,p]]

Description:

Controls the line width and spacing of a printer attached to a parallel port.

LPT*n* is the name of the parallel printer port (LPT1, LPT2, or LPT3). You *must* specify a printer port.

chars is the number of characters to print per line (80 or 132). The default is 80. If you omit *chars*, Mode leaves the current width unchanged.

lines is the number of lines per inch (6 or 8). The default is 6. You must precede *lines* by a comma whether or not you include *chars*. If you omit *lines*, Mode leaves the current spacing unchanged.

p causes DOS to continually retry to send output if the printer is not ready. To stop the retry loop, press Ctrl-Break.

This command is available in all versions of PC-DOS and in MS-DOS versions 3.2 and 3.3.

Example:

To set the spacing of LPT2 to 132 characters per line, leave the line spacing unchanged, and specify continuous retries, type:

```
mode lpt2:132,,p
```

Mode: Configure Serial Port

Syntax:

mode COM*m*[:]*baud*[,*parity*[,*databits*[,*stopbits*[,p]]]]

Description:

Controls the parameters of the serial communications port that define the speed and form of the data transmitted.

COM*m* is the name of the communications port (COM1 or COM2).

baud is the number of bits per second to be sent or received (110, 150, 300, 600, 1200, 2400, 4800, or 9600). You can abbreviate to the first two numbers (for example, 12=1200). In version 3.3, you can specify 19200 if your system is capable of handling such speed. You *must* specify a value for *baud*.

parity is the kind of error-checking technique used (n for none, o for odd, and e for even). The default is e.

databits is the number of bits required to define a character (7 or 8). The default is 7.

stopbits is the number of bits that mark the end of a character (1 or 2). The default is 2 if baud is 110; otherwise, the default is 1.

p causes DOS to continuously retry to send output if the printer is not ready. To stop the retry loop, press Ctrl-Break.

If you omit an optional parameter (except p), you must still type the comma that precedes it; in that case, DOS assumes the default setting for the omitted parameter. (*baud* without any other parameters requires no commas.)

This command is available in all versions of PC-DOS and in MS-DOS versions 3.2 and 3.3.

Example:

To set *baud* for COM2 to 300, *parity* to odd, leave *databits* at 7, and set *stopbits* at 2, type:

```
mode com2:300,o,,2
```

Mode: Redirect Parallel Printer Output

Syntax:

mode LPT*n*[:]=COM*m*[:]

Description:

Redirects the output that would normally go to a printer attached to a parallel port to a printer attached to a serial port.

LPT*n* is the name of the parallel printer port whose output is to be redirected (LPT1, LPT2, or LPT3). If you want to cancel any redirection you applied to that port with a previous Mode: Redirect Parallel Printer Output command, enter LPT*n* alone.

COM*m* is the name of the serial communications port (COM1 or COM2) to which output is to be redirected.

Note: Before you can use this form of Mode, you must use a Mode: Configure Serial Port command.

This command is available in all versions of PC-DOS and in MS-DOS versions 3.2 and 3.3.

Examples:

To redirect printer output from LPT2 to serial port COM2, type:

```
mode lpt2:=com2:
```

To cancel the redirection and restore the printer output to LPT2, type:

```
mode lpt2:
```

Mode: Select Display

Syntax:

mode *display*

Description:

Selects the active display and controls the number of characters per line and whether or not color is used on a display attached to the Color/Graphics Adapter.

display is one of the following values:

mono	Monochrome Display Adapter, 80 columns
40	Color/Graphics Adapter, 40 columns, color unchanged
80	Color/Graphics Adapter, 80 columns, color unchanged
bw40	Color/Graphics Adapter, 40 columns, color disabled
bw80	Color/Graphics Adapter, 80 columns, color disabled
co40	Color/Graphics Adapter, 40 columns, color enabled
co80	Color/Graphics Adapter, 80 columns, color enabled

This form of the Mode command automatically clears the screen.

This command is available in all versions of PC-DOS and in MS-DOS versions 3.2 and 3.3.

Example:

To display 40 columns and enable color on a color display attached to the Color/Graphics Adapter, type:

```
mode co40
```

More

Syntax:

```
more
```

Description:

Reads lines of text from standard input (by default, the keyboard), passes 23 lines to standard output (by default, the video display), displays a line that says -- *More* --, and waits for a key to be pressed before passing the next 23 lines; used to review long files or output from commands one screenful at a time.

Because the input and output of the More command can be redirected, input can also come from a file, a device other than the keyboard, or the output from another command. Likewise, you can redirect the output of the More command to a file or to a device other than the video display.

Example:

To display the file REPORT.TXT one screenful at a time, type:

```
type report.txt ¦ more
```

National Language Support Function

Syntax:

nlsfunc [[*drive:*][*path*]*filename*]

Description:

Tells DOS the name and location of the file that contains country-specific information, such as date and time formats and currency symbols. You must use the Nlsfunc command before you can use the Change Code Page (Chcp) command.

drive:path is the location of the file containing the country-specific information. If you omit both of these, Nlsfunc looks in the root directory of the current drive.

filename is the name of the country-specific information file, which in most versions of MS-DOS is COUNTRY.SYS. If you omit *filename*, Nlsfunc assumes the file is the one specified in the Country configuration command in CONFIG.SYS; if there is no Country configuration command in CONFIG.SYS, Nlsfunc assumes that the file is named COUNTRY.SYS and is located in the root directory of the current drive.

Example:

To specify C:\DOS\COUNTRY.SYS as the country information file, type:

```
nlsfunc c:\dos\country.sys
```

Path

Syntax:

path [[*drive:*][*path*][;[*drive:*][*path*] . . .]]

Description:

Tells DOS where to look for a command file (a file with a .EXE, .COM, or .BAT extension).

drive: is the drive to be searched. If you omit *drive:*, DOS assumes the current drive.

path is the name of the directory or subdirectory to be searched. If you include *drive:* but omit *path*, DOS assumes the current directory of *drive:*.

You can enter more than one *drive:*, *path*, or *drive:path* combination by separating them with semicolons.

A Path command followed only by a semicolon removes any search paths previously set with Path.

A Path command with no parameters displays the current search path for command files.

Example:

To set the search path for command files to include the \DOS and \WORD directories on drive C and the \REPORTS directory on drive A, type:

```
path c:\dos;c:\word;a:\reports
```

Print

Syntax:

print [/d:*device*][/b:*bufsize*][/u:*busytick*][/m:*maxtick*][/s:*timeslice*] [/q:*size*][/t][/c][/p] [*drive:*][*pathname*]

Description:

Prints files while the system is doing something else. Lets you maintain a list, called the print queue, that holds the names of a maximum of 32 files to be printed.

/d:*device* tells Print the printer to use. If you omit /d:*device*, Print prompts you to enter one. The default is PRN. (Not available in versions 2.X.)

/b:*bufsize* sets the size, in bytes, of the internal buffer. This determines the amount of data Print can read from a file at one time. The range is 512 through 16384, and the default is 512. (Not available in versions 2.X.)

/u:*busytick* is the number of timer ticks that Print waits for a busy printer before giving up its time slice. The range is 1 through 255, and the default is 1. (Not available in versions 2.X and MS-DOS version 3.2.)

/m:*maxtick* is the number of timer ticks for which Print keeps control during each of its time slices. The range is 1 through 255, and the default is 2. (Not available in versions 2.X and MS-DOS version 3.2.)

/s:*timeslice* sets the number of time slices per second during which Print is given control of the system. The range is 1 through 255, and the default is 8. (Not available in versions 2.X and in MS-DOS version 3.2.)

/q:*size* tells Print the number of files the print queue can hold. The range is 1 through 32, and the default is 10. (Not available in versions 2.X.)

/t stops all printing. If a document is being printed, printing stops, the paper is advanced to the top of the next page, and all files are removed from the print queue.

/c removes *pathname* from the print queue. If the document is being printed, printing stops and the paper is advanced to the top of the next page.

/p adds *pathname* to the print queue. Print assumes this parameter if all you specify in the command line is *pathname*.

drive:pathname is the name and location of the file to be added to or deleted from the print queue. You can specify a list of files by separating the names with spaces. Wildcard characters are permitted.

Note: In versions 2.X *drive:pathname* must precede the switches; in all other versions the switches must come first.

If you enter the Print command with no parameters, Print displays the list of files in the print queue.

The /b:*bufsize*, /d:*device*, /q:*size*, /m:*maxtick*, /s:*timeslice*, and /u:*busytick* switches configure Print and should be used only the first time it is entered.

Note: Print stops printing a file after encountering a Control-Z character. Therefore, any file containing a ^Z character might not print in its entirely. To print such a file use Copy: Copy a File to a Device and include the /b switch.

Note: You cannot use the Print command with a drive affected by an Assign command.

Examples:

To print the file REPORT.TXT, be sure your printer is turned on and type:

```
print report.txt
```

If you decide you don't want to print REPORT.TXT but would like to print JUNE.RPT, type:

```
print report.txt /c june.rpt /p
```

Prompt

Syntax:

prompt *string*

Description:

Changes the system prompt to *string*.

string is the prompt that is to replace the system prompt.

You can enter any character string you want, or you can enter one of the following $*x* combinations to produce certain characters or useful information:

$*x* Code	*Resulting Display*
$$	The $ character
$t	The time
$d	The date
$p	The current drive and directory
$v	The DOS version number
$n	The current drive
$g	The > character
$l	The < character
$b	The ¦ character
$q	The = character
$h	A backspace; the previous character is erased
$e	The Escape character
$_	Beginning of a new line on the display screen

Note: Any spaces entered between strings or between $x combinations are displayed on the screen.

Prompt without *string* restores the default system prompt.

This command is not available in PC-DOS version 2.0.

Examples:

To define the system prompt as two lines that show the date and the current drive and directory followed by a greater-than sign, type:

```
prompt $d$_$p$g
```

To restore the system prompt to its standard form, simply type:

```
prompt
```

Recover Files

Syntax:

recover [*drive:*]*pathname*
or
recover *drive:*

Description:

Reconstructs a file from a disk that has bad sectors or reconstructs all files from a disk that has a damaged directory structure.

drive:pathname is the name and location of the file containing unreadable sectors to be reconstructed. Wildcard characters are not permitted. If you omit *drive:*, Recover assumes the current drive. To reconstruct an entire disk with a bad directory structure, use *drive:* without a *pathname*.

Recover names recovered files in the form FILE*nnnn*.REC, starting with FILE0001.REC. When reconstructing an entire disk, Recover does not restore subdirectories, although it does reconstruct any files contained in existing subdirectories on the disk with the damaged directory.

Note: Do not use Recover with a drive affected by the Join or Substitute commands. You cannot use Recover with a drive assigned to a network.

Examples:

To reconstruct the file REPORT.TXT from the disk in drive B that has bad sectors, type:

```
recover b:report.txt
```

To reconstruct all files from the disk in drive B that has a bad directory structure, type:

```
recover b:
```

Remove Directory

Syntax:

rmdir [*drive:*]*path*

Description:

Removes (deletes) a directory. (Can be abbreviated rd.)

drive: is the drive that contains the disk with the directory to be removed. If you omit *drive:*, Rmdir assumes that the directory is on the disk in the current drive.

path is the name of the directory to be removed. The directory must not contain files or have any subdirectories. You *must* specify *path* because Rmdir cannot remove the current directory.

Example:

To remove the \LETTERS directory from a directory called \ENG, type:

```
rd \eng\letters
```

Rename

Syntax:

rename [*drive:*]*pathname filename*

Description:

Changes the name of a file. (Can be abbreviated ren.)

drive:pathname is the current name and location of the file to be renamed.

filename is the new name to be given to the file. Wildcard characters are permitted in both names. You cannot precede *filename* with a drive or path; the newly named file is left in the same directory of the same drive.

If *pathname* doesn't exist or another file with the same name as *filename* already exists in that directory, Rename displays an error message and returns to command level.

Examples:

To change the name of the file ANNUAL.BGT to FINAL.BGT on the disk in the current drive, type:

```
rename annual.bgt final.bgt
```

To change all files in the current drive and directory with a .DOC extension to .TXT, type:

```
rename *.doc *.txt
```

Replace

Syntax:

replace [*drive1:*]*pathname* [*drive2:*][*path*] [/a][/d][/p][/r][/s][/w]

Description:

Selectively adds or replaces files on a disk so that you can update the destination disk with more recent versions of files from the source disk.

drive1:pathname specifies the source of the new file(s). Wildcard characters are permitted.

drive2:path specifies the destination location of the file(s).

/a transfers only source files that do not exist at the destination. Cannot be used with /s or /d.

/d replaces only source files with a more recent date than their destination counterparts. Cannot be used with /a. (Available only in MS-DOS version 3.2.)

/p prompts for confirmation before each file is transferred.

/r specifies that destination files marked read-only can be overwritten.

/s searches all subdirectories of the destination directory for a match with the source files. Cannot be used with /a.

/w causes Replace to wait for the user to press any key before transferring files, allowing disks to be changed.

This command is available only in versions 3.2 and 3.3.

Examples:

To replace all files on the disk in drive B with any newer versions of the same files from the \PROGRAMS directory on the disk in drive A, type:

```
replace a:\programs\*.* b:
```

To transfer only files from the disk in drive A that do not already exist on the disk in drive B, type:

```
replace a:*.* b: /a
```

Restore

Syntax:

restore *drive1:* [*drive2:*][*pathname*] [/s][/p][/b:*date*][/a:*date*][/e:*time*] [/L:*time*][/m][/n]

Description:

Restores files that were backed up with the Backup command.

drive1: is the drive that contains the backup floppy disk. You *must* include *drive1:*.

drive2: is the drive to which you are restoring the file or files. If you omit *drive2:*, the file is restored to the current drive.

pathname is the directory to which you are restoring the file and the name of the file, including its extension. Wildcard characters are permitted. If you specify a directory, you *must* also specify a filename.

If you omit *pathname* entirely, all files that were backed up from the current directory are restored on *drive2:*. If you specify only a filename, DOS restores that file to the current directory on *drive2:*. You *must* specify either *drive2:* or *pathname*.

/s restores all files in the subdirectories of the specified directory.

/p prompts for confirmation before restoring hidden files, read-only files, or files that were changed since they were last backed up.

/b:*date* restores files modified on or before *date*. The date format depends on whether the Country command is in effect; the default is *mm-dd-yy*.

/a:*date* restores files modified on or after *date*.

/e:*time* restores files modified at or before *time*. The time format depends on whether the Country command is in effect; the default is *hh:mm:ss*.

/L:*time* restores files modified at or after *time*.

/m restores only files modified since the last backup.

/n restores only files that do not exist on the destination disk.

Versions of PC-DOS prior to 3.3 support only the /s and /p switches.

PC-DOS versions 3.0 and later and MS-DOS versions 3.1 and later support all media combinations.

Note: Version 3.3 does not restore the system files (IBMBIO.COM and IBMDOS.COM for PC-DOS; IO.SYS and MSDOS.SYS for MS-DOS; and COMMAND.COM for both PC-DOS and MS-DOS). You must use the System command and then the Copy command for COMMAND.COM to restore these files.

Example:

To restore all the files on drive A backed up from the \MKT\WP directory on drive B, type:

```
restore a: b:\mkt\wp\*.*
```

Select

Syntax:

select [[a: | b:] *drive:*[*path*]] *nnn xx*

Description:

Formats and configures a country-specific and language-specific system floppy disk that includes a CONFIG.SYS file containing the appropriate Country command and an AUTOEXEC.BAT file containing the appropriate Keyboard command.

a: or b: is the source drive containing the files needed to make the country-specific and language-specific floppy disk. If you omit this parameter, Select assumes drive A.

drive:path is the location of the disk to be formatted and configured for the specified country and the name of the directory for the command files. If you omit this parameter, Select assumes drive B, and the files are placed in the root directory.

nnn is the country code that determines the date and time format after the system is booted with the new disk.

xx is the keyboard code that determines the layout of the keyboard after the system is booted with the new disk.

All country codes and keyboard codes are in the following table:

Country	Country code	Keyboard code
Australia	061	US
Belgium	032	BE
Canada (English)	001	US
Canada (French)	002	CF
Denmark	045	DK
Finland	358	SU
France†	033	FR
Germany†	049	GR
International (English)	061	-
Israel	972	-
Italy†	039	IT
Latin America	003	LA
Middle East (Arabic)	785	-
Netherlands	031	NL
Norway	047	NO
Portugal	351	PO
Spain†	034	SP

† These are the only choices available in PC-DOS versions 3.0 and 3.1.

(continued)

Country	Country code	Keyboard code
Sweden	046	SV
Switzerland (French)	041	SF
Switzerland (German)	041	SG
United Kingdom†	044	UK
United States†	001	US

† These are the only choices available in PC-DOS versions 3.0 and 3.1.

In versions prior to 3.2, you can specify only *nnn* and *xx* in the command line.

In versions 3.2 and later, if *drive:* is a fixed disk, you are prompted to enter the current volume label of the fixed disk. If the volume label you enter does not match the existing volume label of the fixed disk, Select terminates.

This command is available in PC-DOS versions 3.0 and later and in MS-DOS version 3.3.

Examples:

To create a system disk configured for use in West Germany using PC-DOS prior to version 3.2, place a copy of the original distribution disk in drive A and a blank disk in drive B; then type:

```
select 049 gr
```

(If you have a single-drive system, Select prompts you to change disks.)

To create a system disk configured for use in West Germany using PC-DOS version 3.2, place a copy of the original distribution disk in drive A and a blank disk in drive B; then type:

```
select a: b: 049 gr
```

Set Environment Variable

Syntax:

set [*string*=[*value*]]

Description:

Defines an environment variable name and its value. (An environment variable associates a value consisting of filenames, pathnames, or other data with a short symbolic name that can be easily referenced by programs.)

string is the name of the environment variable.

value is the string of characters, pathnames, or filenames that defines the current value of *string*.

If you omit *value*, Set deletes the environment variable name from the environment. If you omit all parameters, Set displays all the variables in the environment.

Example:

To inform the Microsoft C Compiler that it can find *include* files in the \INCLUDE directory on drive B, type:

```
set include=b:\include
```

Share

Syntax:

share [/f:*space*][/L:*locks*]

Description:

Loads into the system's memory a module that supports file sharing and locking in a networking environment.

/f:*space* specifies memory allocation, in bytes, for holding file-sharing information. (The default is 2048.)

/L:*locks* specifies the number of file region locks. (The default is 20).

This command is available only in versions 3.0 and later.

Examples:

To load Share into memory using the default values, simply type:

```
share
```

To adjust the memory to 4096 bytes and the file region locks to 40, type:

```
share /f:4096 /L:40
```

Sort

Syntax:

sort [*drive:*][*pathname*] [/r][/+*n*]

Description:

Sorts lines you enter at the keyboard and sends them to the display; also can be used with redirection characters as a filter to sort the contents of a file or the output of another program.

drive:pathname is the name and location of a file to be sorted and must be preceded by the < redirection character. If you omit *drive:*, Sort assumes the current drive. If you omit *drive:pathname*, keyboard input is sorted. (Keyboard input must be terminated with F6 or Ctrl-Z.)

/r sorts lines in reverse order (from Z to A).

/+*n* sorts lines starting with the contents in column *n*. (The default is 1.)

Sort does not distinguish between uppercase and lowercase.

Examples:

To sort a file called PHONE.TXT in drive B in ascending order based on the character in column 37, type:

```
sort < b:phone.txt /+37
```

To sort a directory listing in reverse alphabetic order, type:

```
dir ¦ sort /r
```

Substitute

Syntax:

subst [*drive1: drive2:path*]
or
subst *drive1:* /d

Description:

Lets you access a directory by a drive letter. After the substitution, DOS automatically replaces any reference to *drive1:* with *drive2:path*.

drive1: is the letter to be used instead of *drive2:path*.

drive2:path is the drive and path that you want to refer to.

/d cancels any substitution in effect for *drive1:*.

If you enter Substitute without any parameters, Substitute displays a list of substitutions in effect.

This command is available only in versions 3.1 and later.

The following commands do not work on drives affected by the Substitute command:

Assign	Fdisk
Chkdsk	Format
Diskcomp	Label
Diskcopy	Recover
Fastopen	System

Examples:

To reference the path \MPLAN\SALES\FORECAST on drive C by the drive letter D, type:

```
subst d: c:\mplan\sales\forecast
```

To cancel the substitution, type:

```
subst d: /d
```

System

Syntax:

sys *drive:*

Description:

Transfers the DOS system files from the disk in the default drive to the disk in the specified drive.

drive: is the drive containing the disk to be copied to. The disk must be formatted but completely empty. (See Format.)

Note: In version 3.3, the system files need not be contiguous. Therefore, you do not have to format the disk in *drive:* if you want to use the Sys command to copy version 3.3 onto a disk containing versions 3.2 or earlier. (You cannot use Sys to copy PC-DOS version 3.3 system files to a disk containing an older version of MS-DOS or vice-versa.)

After completion of the Sys operation, you can make the disk a bootable disk by copying the file COMMAND.COM to the new disk.

Note: Do not use System with a drive affected by the Join or Substitute commands. The System command ignores drive reassignments made with the Assign command. You cannot use System with a drive assigned to a network.

Example:

To transfer the DOS system files to the disk in drive B, type:

```
sys b:
```

Time

Syntax:

time [*hh*:*mm*[:*ss*[.*xx*]]]

Description:

Sets the system clock.

hh is the hours, based on a 24-hour clock (0 through 23, where 0 is midnight).

mm is the minutes (0 through 59). If you do not include *mm* and specify only *hh*, DOS sets *mm* to 00.

ss is the seconds (0 through 59). This value is optional.

xx is hundredths of a second (0 through 99). This value is optional. If you include it, you must specify *ss*.

No spaces are allowed between any of the parameters.

If you don't include any parameters, Time displays the current setting of the system clock and prompts you to enter the time. If you do not want to change the time, simply press Enter.

You can change the time format by using the Country command in the CONFIG.SYS file. (See Country.)

Example:

To set the time to 8:15 PM, type:

```
time 20:15
```

Tree

Syntax:

tree [*drive:*] [/f]

Description:

Displays the path and, optionally, lists the contents of each directory and subdirectory on a disk.

drive: is the drive whose directory structure is to be displayed. If you omit *drive:*, Tree displays the directory structure of the current drive.

/f displays the name of each file in the root directory and in each directory and subdirectory.

This command is available in all versions of PC-DOS and in MS-DOS versions 3.2 and 3.3.

Example:

Suppose the disk in drive B contains many files stored in various directories. To find out which files are stored in which directories, type:

```
tree b: /f
```

Type

Syntax:

type [*drive:*]*pathname*

Description:

Displays the contents of a file.

drive:pathname is the name and location of the file to be displayed. Wildcard characters are not permitted. If you omit *drive:*, Type assumes the file is on the disk in the current drive.

If the file you name doesn't exist, Type displays *File not found* and returns to command level.

Note: If you use the Type command to display an executable file (a file with a .EXE or .COM extension) or a binary file created by an application, you'll probably hear beeps and see unintelligible characters on the screen including graphics symbols. You cannot view such files with the Type command.

Example:

To display the contents of REPORT.JAN located in the REPORTS directory on the current drive, type:

```
type \reports\report.jan
```

Verify

Syntax:

verify [on | off]

Description:

Turns on or off an internal switch that controls disk write verification.

If Verify is on, DOS checks that the data was written correctly to disk (no bad sectors).

If you enter no parameters, Verify displays the current status of the verify switch. The default condition is off.

Example:

To turn the verify switch on, type:

```
verify on
```

Version

Syntax:

ver

Description:

Displays the version number of DOS being used.

Example:

To determine which version of DOS you are currently running, type:

```
ver
```

Version replies with the full name and number.

Volume

Syntax:

vol [*drive:*]

Description:

Displays the volume label assigned to the specified disk, if one exists.

drive: is the drive that contains the disk whose volume label is to be displayed. If you omit *drive:*, Volume displays the volume label of the disk in the current drive.

Example:

To display the volume label of the disk in drive B, type:

```
vol b:
```

Xcopy (Extended Copy)

Syntax:

xcopy [*drive:*]*pathname1* [*drive:*][*pathname2*] [/a][/d:*date*][/e][/m][/p] [/s][/v][/w]

Description:

Copies files. Optionally copies directories and their subdirectories, if they exist.

drive:pathname1 is the name and location of the source file. If you specify only a drive, Xcopy copies all files in the current directory of the specified drive. If you specify only a path without a filename, Xcopy copies all files from the specified path on the current drive. You must specify at least one of the source parameters.

drive:pathname2 is the name and location of the target file. Wildcard characters are permitted in both filenames. If you do not specify a destination, Xcopy assumes the current directory of the current drive.

If you specify a drive other than the current drive for *pathname1* and omit *drive:pathname2*, *pathname1* is copied to the current directory of the current drive. If you specify only a drive for *pathname2*, *pathname1* is copied to the disk in the drive you specify and given the same filename.

/a copies source files that have their archive bit set. It does not modify the archive bit of the source file.

/d:*date* copies source files modified on or after the date specified. The date format depends on whether the Country command is in effect; the default is *mm-dd-yy*.

/e copies subdirectories even if they are empty. You must use this switch with the /s switch.

/m copies source files that have their archive bit set and then turns off the archive bit in the source file.

/p prompts you to confirm whether you want to create each destination file.

/s copies directories and their subdirectories, unless they are empty. If you omit this switch, Xcopy works within a single directory.

/v verifies each file as it is written to the target to ensure that the target files are identical to the source files.

/w causes Xcopy to wait for you to press a key before it starts the copy process, allowing you to change disks.

This command is available only in versions 3.2 and 3.3.

Example:

To copy all files, directories, and subdirectories (including the empty ones) from drive A to drive B and verify that all files were copied intact, type:

```
xcopy a:*.* b: /e /s /v
```

BATCH COMMANDS

A batch file is simply a collection of DOS commands. It is a useful way to execute a series of commands that you use frequently or to perform simple programming tasks. In addition to the standard DOS commands, your batch file can include a set of special commands that let you write simple programs, with decision points and replaceable parameters. (A replaceable parameter, an integer between 0 and 9 preceded by a % symbol, is replaced by arguments you type in the command line when you invoke the batch file.) One of the most commonly used batch files is the AUTOEXEC.BAT file that DOS reads whenever you start up or reboot your system. This file might let you enter the current date, select the display colors, and load a program, without having to type each of these commands separately. AUTOEXEC.BAT must be located in the root directory of the disk you boot DOS from.

You can create or modify a batch file with any word processor capable of creating text-only (ASCII) files or with Edlin, the DOS text editor. Simply type in the DOS commands in order of execution and then save the file. All batch files must have the extension .BAT, although the extension need not be typed on the command line when you run the file.

To execute a batch file, simply type its name at the system prompt. DOS then sequentially performs the commands it contains.

The following file, ARCHIVE.BAT, demonstrates the use of batch commands. The program copies files from drive B to the \BAK directory on drive C. It first turns Echo off and clears the screen and then checks to see if you typed any filenames on the command line. If you didn't, the program displays a message and stops. Otherwise, it prompts you to put a disk in drive B and press a key when you're ready to continue; then it sequentially copies the files you included after the batch file name.

```
@echo off
cls
rem At the command prompt, type the
rem batch file name followed by the
```

(continued)

```
rem names of the files on drive B
rem that you want stored in the \BAK
rem directory on drive C.
if not "%1"=="" goto start
echo You must follow ARCHIVE with a
echo list of files!
goto end
:start
echo Insert the disk containing the
echo files to archive in drive B.
pause
:loop
for %%f in (b:%1) do copy %%f c:\bak
shift
if not exist b:%1 goto end
goto loop
:end
```

To execute ARCHIVE.BAT and store the files PROG1.C, PROG2.C, and PROG3.C from the disk in drive B to the \BAK directory on drive C, type:

```
archive prog1.c prog2.c prog3.c
```

@

Syntax:

@ command

Description:

Prevents commands in a batch file from being displayed when DOS executes them. (Available only in version 3.3.)

command is any DOS command line. The @ symbol must precede *command*.

A common use of the @ symbol is to hide the first *echo off* statement in a batch file.

Call

Syntax:

call [*drive:*][*path*]*batchfile* [*parameters*]

Description:

Lets you carry out the commands in a second batch file and then return to the original batch file and continue with the next command. This lets you use a batch command you create exactly as you would use any other DOS command. (Available only in version 3.3.)

drive:path is the location of *batchfile*. If you omit *drive:* or path, DOS assumes the current drive or path. If you omit both, DOS assumes the current drive and directory.

batchfile is the name of the batch file you want DOS to execute.

parameters represents any parameters that *batchfile* requires. You can either enter the parameters themselves, or you can use replaceable parameters so that parameters sent to the current batch file are passed along to the batch file being called.

Echo

Syntax:

echo [on ¦ off ¦ *message*]

Description:

Controls whether commands in a batch file are displayed as they are carried out. Also lets you display your own messages.

If you specify Echo on (the default), commands are displayed; if you specify Echo off, they are not.

message specifies your own message and is displayed even if you have previously set Echo off. If Echo is on, the word *echo* is displayed in front of the message. To display a blank line on the screen with versions 2.X, type a space after the Echo command and press Enter.

To display a blank line with versions 3.X, type a space after Echo, hold down the Alt key, and press 255 on the numeric keypad; finally, release the Alt key and press Enter.

If you omit all options, DOS tells you whether Echo is on or off.

For

Syntax:

for *%%variable* in (*set*) do *command*

Description:

Allows you to carry out a DOS command on one or more files.

%%variable is the name of a variable that is assigned, in turn, each value in *set*. The name should not be any of the numerals 0 through 9.

set is the list of filenames (or replaceable parameters representing file-names) that are sequentially assigned to *%%variable*. You must separate the filenames or parameters with spaces and enclose the entire list in parentheses. Wildcard characters are permitted.

command is any DOS command other than the For command and can include both replaceable parameters (such as %1) representing file-names specified in the command line and the For command's own replaceable parameter (*%%variable*). (See the example at the beginning of this section for the use of replaceable parameters.)

Goto

Syntax:

goto *label*

Description:

Tells DOS to go to a specific line in the batch file, rather than to the next command in the sequence, and resume execution.

label is a string that identifies the line in the batch file where DOS is to resume execution. *label* must appear on a line by itself and begin with a colon.

If

Syntax:

if [not] *condition command*

Description:

Checks whether a condition is true. If it is, DOS carries out the specified command, unless you include the parameter word *not*, in which case DOS carries out the command if the condition is not true.

condition is the condition to be evaluated and takes one of three forms:

errorlevel *number*	True if the previous program executed by COMMAND.COM had an exit code of *number* or higher.
string1==string2	True when *string1* and *string2* are identical. Uppercase or lowercase is significant.
exist *filename*	True if *filename* exists. You can include a drive and path, and wildcard characters are permitted.

command is any DOS command and can include replaceable parameters (such as %1) representing parameters specified in the command line. (See the example at the beginning of this section for use of replaceable parameters.)

Pause

Syntax:

pause [*message*]

Description:

Causes DOS to pause, display the line *Strike a key when ready...*, and wait for you to press any key, giving you time to read a message or complete such preparations as turning on your printer or changing disks. Also lets you display your own message.

message is a string of characters containing your own message, such as a reminder or a warning. It is displayed only if Echo is on.

Remark

Syntax:

rem [*message*]

Description:

Displays a message if Echo is on; lets you include hidden explanatory notes in your batch files if Echo is off.

message is a string of characters containing your message or comments. If you do not want comments displayed on your screen, you must include Echo off at the beginning of your batch file or precede the *rem* command with the @ symbol. (@ is available only in version 3.3.)

Shift

Syntax:

shift

Description:

Discards the contents of the %0 replaceable parameter (the parameter containing the batch file name) and shifts the contents of each subsequent parameter to a lower number. (%1 becomes %0, %2 becomes %1, and so on.)

Batch files can handle only 10 replaceable parameters (%0 through %9) at a time. By moving an eleventh parameter into %9, Shift lets you specify more than 10 arguments in the command line. You can use Shift as often as necessary to process all arguments. With each shift, the current contents of %0 are lost and cannot be recovered.

CONFIGURATION COMMANDS

Unlike other DOS commands, which tell DOS *what* to do, configuration commands tell DOS *how* to do something, such as use a device or communicate with a disk drive. You will need these commands infrequently, usually only when you add a device to your computer system (thereby changing its *configuration*).

Configuration commands are not typed at the keyboard; you put them in a special file called CONFIG.SYS that must be in the root directory of the DOS disk you use to boot the system. DOS carries out these commands only when it is started; therefore, if you change a command in CONFIG.SYS, you must restart DOS for the command to take effect.

Some application programs require you to add certain commands to the CONFIG.SYS file so that the application can run properly; for example, an application may require that DOS be able to work with more than the eight files it is able to work with by default.

You can create or modify a CONFIG.SYS file with any word processor that can create text-only (ASCII) files or with Edlin, the DOS text editor. You can add or change any of the configuration commands explained in this section. Each command must be on a separate line, as shown in the following example:

```
break=on
buffers=20
country=049
device=c:\dos\ansi.sys
device=mouse.sys
drivparm=/d:1 /s:9 /t:80
fcbs=8,4
files=20
lastdriv=z
shell=c:\dos\command.com
stacks=8,512
```

Break

Syntax:

break=[on ¦ off]

Description:

Instructs DOS how often to check for a Ctrl-C (or Ctrl-Break), the key sequence you use to terminate a program or batch file.

By default, DOS checks for Ctrl-C each time it reads from or writes to a character device (screen, printer, or serial port). If Break is on, DOS also checks for Ctrl-C each time a disk is read from or written to.

Buffers

Syntax:

buffers=*number*

Description:

Defines the number of work areas in memory that DOS uses to store data when reading from and writing to disk.

number is the number of buffers you need (1 through 99). Unless you instruct otherwise, *number* is 2 (3 for the IBM PC/AT).

In version 3.3, *number* can be 2 through 255. The default depends on how your system is configured:

Configuration	Default buffers
Base system	2
Floppy disk drive > 360 KB	3
128 KB to 255 KB RAM	5
256 KB to 511 KB RAM	10
512 KB RAM or more	15

Note: Buffers require memory, so you should avoid specifying a number greater than 30.

Country

Syntax:

country=*nnn*[,[*codepage*][,[*drive:*]*filename*]]

Description:

Tells DOS to follow local conventions for a given country in such matters as date format, currency symbols, and decimal separators. If you do not specify a country, DOS follows the conventions for the country for which DOS was manufactured. This command is available only in versions 3.0 and later.

nnn is a three-digit country code number from the following list. You must include all three digits, including any zeros at the beginning.

Country	Country Code
Arabic	785
Australia	061
Belgium	032
Canada (French)	002
Denmark	045
Finland	358
France	033
Germany	049
Israel	972
Italy	039
Netherlands	031
Norway	047
Portugal	351
Spain	034
Sweden	046
Switzerland	041
United Kingdom	044
United States	001

codepage is a three-digit number that specifies the code page that DOS is to use. (Available only in version 3.3.)

Code Page	Code-Page Number
United States	437
Multilingual	850
Portuguese	860
French Canadian	863
Nordic	865

drive:filename is the name and location of the file supplied with your DOS disks that contains country-specific information. If you omit *drive:*, DOS assumes the file is stored in the root directory of the disk used to boot the system. If you omit *filename*, DOS assumes the file is COUNTRY.SYS. (Available only in version 3.3.)

Device

Syntax:

device=[*drive:*]*pathname*

Description:

Specifies a device driver program (a file with the extension .SYS) that tells DOS how to use a particular device, such as a Microsoft Mouse.

drive: is the drive on which the program exists. If you omit *drive:*, DOS assumes the program is on the disk used to boot the system.

pathname is the directory location and name of the program—for example, \DEVICE\MOUSE.SYS for the Microsoft Mouse driver located in the \DEVICE directory.

If you have more than one device driver to install, you can use more than one device= command in your CONFIG.SYS file.

These device driver programs are normally included with DOS: ANSI.SYS (only in versions 2.0 and later), DISPLAY.SYS (only in version 3.3), PRINTER.SYS (only in version 3.3), and RAMDRIVE.SYS (only in MS-DOS versions 3.2 and 3.3). PC-DOS versions 3.0 and later contain the VDISK.SYS device driver.

Drivparm

Syntax:

drivparm=/d:*dd*[/c][/f:*ff*][/h:*hh*][/n][/s:*ss*][/t:*tt*]

Description:

Alters the system's table of characteristics for a specific block device, overriding the default DOS characteristics. (Whenever a device such as a disk drive performs input or output, it refers to an internal table of characteristics for that device.)

/d:*dd* designates the drive number *dd*. (The valid range is 0 through 255, where 0=drive A, 1=drive B, and so on.)

/c indicates that the device requires change-line (doorlock) support.

/f:*ff* designates one of these device types. (The default value is 2.)

0	5.25-inch 320 KB or 360 KB floppy disk
1	5.25-inch 1.2 MB floppy disk
2	3.5-inch 720 KB floppy disk
3	8-inch single-density floppy disk
4	8-inch double-density floppy disk
5	Fixed disk
6	Tape drive
7	3.5-inch 1.44 MB floppy disk

/h:*hh* indicates the number of read/write heads. (The valid range is 1 through 99; the default value is 2.)

/n indicates that the device is not removable.

/s:*ss* designates the number of sectors per track. (The valid range is 1 through 99; the default value is 9.)

/t:*tt* designates the number of tracks per side. (The valid range is 1 through 99.)

You can include multiple Drivparm commands (each modifying the characteristics for a different device) in the same CONFIG.SYS file.

This command is available only in MS-DOS versions 3.2 and 3.3.

Fcbs (File Control Blocks)

Syntax:

fcbs=*x,y*

Description:

Tells DOS the maximum number of files that can be open at the same time using file control blocks (FCBs). (FCBs are data structures that reside in an application's memory space and store information about open files.) Also tells DOS not to automatically close a certain number of files.

x is the maximum number of files that can be open concurrently using FCBs. (The valid range is 1 through 255; the default is 4.)

y is the number of files opened with FCBs, counting from the first file, that are protected against automatic closure. (The valid range is 0 through 255; the default is 0.) When DOS needs to open more files than *x*, it closes the least recently used file to make room for the new file. The first *y* files are not included in the "close" list. *y* must always be less than or equal to *x*.

This command is available only in PC-DOS versions 3.1 and later and in MS-DOS versions 3.0 and later.

Files

Syntax:

files=*number*

Description:

Tells DOS how many files it can have open at one time.

number is the number of files that can be open. (The valid range is 8 through 255; the default is 8.) A practical suggested value is 20.

Lastdrive

Syntax:

lastdrive=*letter*

Description:

Specifies the last drive letter DOS recognizes as valid.

letter is a letter from a through z. If you do not include Lastdrive in a CONFIG.SYS file, the highest drive letter DOS recognizes as valid is e.

This command is available only in versions 3.0 and later.

Shell

Syntax:

shell=[*drive:*]*pathname*

Description:

Defines the name and location of the file that contains the command processor. (The command processor, or shell, is your interface to the operating system. The default shell for DOS is COMMAND.COM.)

drive:pathname is the name and location of the file containing the command processor. Optional or required switches and other parameters for the command processor can follow the filename, although the Shell command itself has no switches or parameters.

DOS automatically loads COMMAND.COM from the root directory of the disk used to boot the system unless the CONFIG.SYS file contains a Shell command. The most common use of the Shell command is to advise DOS that COMMAND.COM is stored in a location other than the root directory.

Stacks

Syntax:

stacks=*number,size*

Description:

Reserves memory within DOS for temporary use during hardware interrupts. The Stacks command is required by some application programs.

number is the number of stacks to be allocated. (The valid range is 0 through 64; the default is 0.)

size is the size of each stack in bytes. (The valid range is 0 through 512; the default is 0.)

This command is available only in versions 3.2 and 3.3.

EDLIN COMMANDS

Edlin is a simple text editor that lets you:

- Create and save new text (ASCII) files.
- Update existing files and save both the updated and original versions.
- Edit, delete, insert, copy, move, and display lines.
- Search for, delete, or replace text.

The text created or edited with Edlin is divided into lines of varying length, up to 253 characters per line. You must press Enter at the end of each line. (If a line is longer than your screen display, it appears as two or more lines on the screen.)

Line numbers are displayed by Edlin as you edit but are not present in the saved file.

To start Edlin, type:

edlin [*drive:*]*pathname* [/b]

drive:pathname is the name and location of an existing file or of a new file to be created with Edlin.

/b causes Control-Z characters in the file to be ignored.

Once you start Edlin, you will see the Edlin command prompt (an asterisk). You can then enter commands to do such tasks as listing existing lines, inserting lines, moving a range of lines, and replacing strings of characters. When you enter the commands described in this section, it makes no difference whether you type spaces between the variables and the letter specifying the command.

Append

Syntax:

[*number*]**a**

Description:

Reads the number of lines specified from disk into memory.

number is the number of lines to be read. If a number is not specified or is too large, Edlin reads in lines until available memory is 75% full. Use this command only after using the Write command.

Append has no effect if available memory is already 75% full.

Copy

Syntax:

[*range*],*line*[,*number*]c

Description:

Copies one or more lines to the position specified.

range is the numbers of the starting and ending lines to be copied, separated by a comma. You must enter the comma within *range* even if you omit one or both of the line numbers. If you omit the starting number, the copied lines start with the current line. If you omit the ending number, the copied lines end with the current line. If you omit both numbers, only the current line is copied.

line is the number of the line before which you want to place the copied lines. The previous contents of *line* and the remainder of the file are pushed ahead and renumbered. The first copied line becomes the current line.

The line numbers in *range* and *line* must not overlap.

number indicates how many times the lines should be copied.

Delete

Syntax:

[*range*]d

Description:

Deletes one or more lines.

range is the numbers of the starting and ending lines to be deleted, separated by a comma. If you omit the starting number, you must precede the ending number with a comma. If you omit the starting number, the deletion starts at the current line and continues to the ending line. If you omit the ending number, only the starting line is deleted. If you omit both numbers, the current line is deleted. The lines following the deleted lines are pushed back and renumbered. The line following the last deleted line becomes the current line.

Edit Line

Syntax:

[*line*]

Description:

Displays a line of text so that you can edit it.

line is the number of the line to be edited. Enter a period (.) to edit the current line.

If you do not want to edit the line, press Enter to leave it unchanged.

End Edit

Syntax:

e

Description:

Stores the edited file and returns to DOS. If you are editing an existing file, this command changes the extension of the original input file to .BAK, overwriting a file with the same name and a .BAK extension, if one exists.

Insert

Syntax:

[*line*]i

Description:

Allows you to insert new lines in the position specified.

line is the number of the line before which you want to insert a line. The previous contents of *line* and the remainder of the file are pushed ahead and renumbered. The line following the last inserted line becomes the current line.

If you are beginning a new Edlin text file or simply want to insert lines before the current line, do not include a line number. To insert lines at the end of a file, specify # for *line*. To stop inserting, press Ctrl-C or Ctrl-Break.

List

Syntax:

[*range*]l

Description:

Displays one or more lines.

range is the numbers of the starting and ending lines to be displayed, separated by a comma. You must enter the comma within *range* if you omit the starting number. If you omit the starting number, the list starts 11 lines before the current line and continues to the ending line. If you omit the ending number, the list contains 23 lines starting with the starting line. If you omit both numbers, the list contains 23 lines centered around the current line. List has no effect on the current line number.

List scrolls through the entire range, without stopping. To pause the screen, press Ctrl-S; when you are ready, press any key to resume scrolling.

Move

Syntax:

[*range*],*line***m**

Description:

Moves one or more lines to the position specified.

range is the numbers of the starting and ending lines to be moved, separated by a comma. You must enter the comma within *range* even if you omit one or both of the numbers. If you omit the starting number, the move starts with the current line. You can substitute a plus sign (+) followed by a number for the ending number to indicate that you want to move the current line plus the specified number of subsequent lines. If you omit the ending number, the move ends with the current line. If you omit both numbers, only the current line is moved.

line is the line before which you want to place the moved lines. The file is automatically renumbered after the move. The first line moved becomes the current line.

The line numbers in *range* and *line* must not overlap.

Page

Syntax:

[*range*]**p**

Description:

Displays one or more lines.

range is the numbers of the starting and ending lines to be displayed, separated by a comma. If you omit the starting number, you must precede the ending number with a comma. If you omit the starting number, the list starts one line past the current line and continues to the ending line. If you omit the ending number, the list contains 23 lines beginning with the starting line. If you omit both numbers, the list is 23 lines starting one line past the current line.

Page differs from List in that it changes the current line to the last line displayed.

Quit

Syntax:

q

Description:

Cancels an editing session and returns to DOS without storing the revised file.

Edlin prompts you for approval before quitting.

Replace

Syntax:

[*range*][?]**r**[*string1*][^Z*string2*]

Description:

Searches for a string and replaces it with a different string.

range is the numbers of the starting and ending lines to be searched, separated by a comma. You must enter the comma within *range* if you omit the starting number. If you omit the starting number, the search starts at one line past the current line. If you omit the ending number, the search continues to the last line. If you omit both numbers, the search starts at one line past the current line and continues to the last line.

? causes Edlin to prompt for confirmation of each change.

· *string1* is the string to be replaced.

string2 is the new string to be substituted. If you omit *string2*, the command deletes *string1*. In this case, you must end the command after *string1* by pressing the Enter key. If you do specify *string2*, you must separate the two strings by pressing F6 or Ctrl-Z.

Example:

To replace the word *document* with the word *report* wherever it occurs in lines 20 through 55, type:

```
20,55rdocument^Zreport
```

Search

Syntax:

[*range*][?]s*string*

Description:

Searches one or more lines for a specified string of characters.

range is the numbers of the starting and ending lines to be searched, separated by a comma. You must enter the comma within *range* if you omit the starting number. If you omit the starting number, the search starts one line past the current line. If you omit the ending number, the search continues to the last line. If you omit both numbers, the search starts one line past the current line and continues to the last line.

? causes Edlin to prompt for confirmation after each occurrence of *string*; respond *n* to continue the search.

string is the string to be searched for. If you type a space after the s, Search considers that part of *string*. The line containing *string* becomes the current line.

Transfer

Syntax:

[*line*]**t**[*drive:*][*path*]*filename*

Description:

Copies (merges) another file into the file you're creating or editing.

line is the number of the line before which you want to place the copied lines. If you omit *line*, Edlin inserts the copy before the current line. The previous contents of *line* and the remainder of the file are pushed ahead and renumbered, and *line* becomes the current line.

drive:filename can include a drive letter, a filename, and an extension. In versions 3.0 and later, you can also include a path.

Write

Syntax:

[*number*]**w**

Description:

Writes the number of lines specified from memory to disk.

number is the number of lines to be written, beginning with line 1. Use this command only when editing a file larger than 75% of available memory. If you omit *number*, lines are written until a total of 25% of memory remains free.

Write has no effect unless memory is at least 75% full.

INDEX

Special Character

@ 64

A

Append (DOS Command) 1–2
Append (Edlin Command) 79–80
Assign 2–3
Attribute 3–4

B

Backup 4–5
Break (Configuration Command) 72
Break (DOS Command) 5–6
Buffers 72

C

Call 65
Change Code Page 6–7
Change Directory 7–8
Check Disk 8
Clear Screen 9
Command Processor 9–10
Compare 10–11
Copy (Edlin Command) 80
Copy: Combine Files 11–12
Copy: Copy from a Device 12
Copy: Copy a File to a Device 13
Copy: Copy a File to a File 13–14
Country 73–74
Ctty (Change I/O Device) 15

D

Date 15–16
Delete (DOS Command) 16
Delete (Edlin Command) 80–81
Device 74
Directory 17
Disk Compare 17–18
Disk Copy 19
Drivparm 75

E

Echo 65–66
Edit Line 81
End Edit 81
Erase 20
Exe2bin (Executable to Binary Conversion) 20–21
Exit 21

F

Fastopen 21–22
Fcbs (File Control Blocks) 76
File Compare 22–23
Files 76
Find 24
Fixed Disk 24–25
For 66
Format 25–26

G

Goto 66–67
Graphics 27–28
Graphics Table 28–29

I

If 67
Insert 82

J

Join 29–30

K

Keyboard 30–32

L

Label 32–33
Lastdrive 77
List 82

M

Make Directory 33
Mode: Align Display (Color/Graphics Adapter) 34
Mode: Codepage Prepare 34–35
Mode: Codepage Refresh 36
Mode: Codepage Select 36–37
Mode: Codepage Status 37
Mode: Configure Printer 37–38
Mode: Configure Serial Port 38–39
Mode: Redirect Parallel Printer Output 39–40
Mode: Select Display 40–41
More 41
Move 83

N

National Language Support Function 42

P

Page 83–84
Path 42–43
Pause 67–68
Print 43–45
Prompt 45–46

Q

Quit 84

R

Recover Files 46–47
Remark 68
Remove Directory 47
Rename 47–48
Replace (DOS Command) 48–49

Replace (Edlin Command) 84–85
Restore 49–50

S

Search 85
Select 50–52
Set Environment Variable 52–53
Share 53–54
Shell 77
Shift 68–69
Sort 54
Stacks 78
Substitute 55
System 56

T

Time 56–57
Transfer 85–86
Tree 57–58
Type 58

V

Verify 58–59
Version 59
Volume 59–60

W

Write 86

X

Xcopy (Extended Copy) 60–61

OTHER TITLES FROM MICROSOFT PRESS

The Quick Reference Series

QUICK REFERENCE GUIDE TO HARD DISK MANAGEMENT
Van Wolverton

Here is all the core information you need to organize, maintain, and troubleshoot your hard-disk problems along with tips on installing secondary hard disks; the necessary PC-DOS and MS-DOS commands for formatting, configuring, and organizing a hard disk; and more.

96 pages, 4³/₄ x 8, softcover $5.95 Order #86-96353

Programmer's Quick Reference Series

IBM® ROM BIOS
Ray Duncan

A handy and compact guide to the ROM BIOS services of IBM PC, PC/AT, and PS/2 machines. Duncan provides you with an overview of each ROM BIOS service along with its required parameters or arguments, its returned results, and version dependencies.

128 pages, 4³/₄ x 8, softcover $5.95 Order #86-96478

RUNNING MS-DOS®, 3rd edition
The Classic, Definitive Work on DOS — Now Completely Revised and Expanded to Include All Versions of PC/MS-DOS® — Including Hard-Disk Management Tips and Techniques
Van Wolverton

"This book is simply the definitive handbook of PC/MS-DOS...written for both novices and experienced users." **BYTE**

Van Wolverton will guide you through hands-on examples of PC-DOS and MS-DOS commands and capabilities. He will also show you how to work with files and directories on a floppy- or hard-disk system; how to effectively manage printers, monitors, and modems; how to automate frequently performed tasks with batch files; and much more. An expanded MS-DOS command reference is included. Covers MS-DOS through version 3.3. RUNNING MS-DOS — accept no substitutes.

512 pages, 7³/₈ x 9¹/₄, softcover $22.95 Order #86-96262
hardcover $35.00 Order #86-96270

SUPERCHARGING MS-DOS®
The Microsoft® Guide to High Performance Computing for the Experienced PC User

Van Wolverton

"SUPERCHARGING MS-DOS is a valuable addition to any PC user's reference library. For advanced MS-DOS users and software programmers it's a must." Microtimes

When you're ready for more power, this sequel to RUNNING MS-DOS provides intermediate- to advanced-level tips on maximizing the power of MS-DOS. Control your screen and keyboard with ANSI.SYS; create, examine, or change any file; and personalize your CONFIG.SYS file. Includes programs and dozens of valuable batch files.

320 pages, 7³/₈ x 9¹/₄, softcover $18.95 Order #86-95595

SUPERCHARGING MS-DOS is also available with a handy 5.25-inch companion disk that contains scores of batch files, script files, and programs from the book. Used in conjunction with the book, the companion disk is a timesaving tool.

SUPERCHARGING MS-DOS®, Software Version

Van Wolverton

**320 pages, softcover with one 5.25-inch disk $34.95
Order #86-96304**

INSIDE OS/2

*Gordon Letwin, Chief Architect, Systems Software, Microsoft
Foreword by Bill Gates*

"Mere recommendations aren't good enough for INSIDE OS/2.... If you're at all serious about OS/2 you must buy this book."

Dr. Dobb's Journal

INSIDE OS/2 is an unprecedented, candid, and exciting technical examination of OS/2. Letwin takes you inside the philosophy, key development issues, programming implications, and future of OS/2. A valuable and revealing programmer-to-programmer discussion. You can't get a more inside view. This is a book no OS/2 programmer can afford to be without!

304 pages, 7³/₈ x 9¹/₄, softcover $19.95 Order #86-96288